HELPING YOURSELF HELPING OTHERS

Dealing with EATING DISORDERS

Kristin Thiel

Cavendish Square
New York

Published in 2020 by Cavendish Square Publishing, LLC
243 5th Avenue, Suite 136, New York, NY 10016

First Edition

Website: cavendishsq.com

Library of Congress Cataloging-in-Publication Data

Names: Thiel, Kristin, 1977- author.
Title: Dealing with eating disorders / Kristin Thiel.
Description: New York : Cavendish Square, 2020. | Series: Helping yourself, helping others |
Audience: Grades 7-12. | Includes bibliographical references and index.
Identifiers: LCCN 2018056045 (print) | LCCN 2018057512 (ebook) | ISBN 9781502646255 (ebook) |
ISBN 9781502646248 (library bound) | ISBN 9781502646231 (pbk.)
Subjects: LCSH: Eating disorders--Juvenile literature. | Eating disorders--Treatment--Juvenile literature.
Classification: LCC RC552.E18 (ebook) | LCC RC552.E18 T44 2020 (print) | DDC 616.85/26--dc23
LC record available at https://lccn.loc.gov/2018056045

Editorial Director: David McNamara
Editor: Caitlyn Miller
Copy Editor: Rebecca Rohan
Associate Art Director: Alan Sliwinski
Designer: Ginny Kemmerer
Production Coordinator: Karol Szymczuk
Photo Research: J8 Media

The photographs in this book are used by permission and through the courtesy of: Cover Foxys Forest Manufacture/Shutterstock.com; p. 4 Monkey Business Images/Shutterstock.com; p. 13 Bob Stone/Conde Nast/Getty Images; p. 14 Josiah Kamau/BuzzFoto/Getty Images; p. 19 Noam Galai/Getty Images; p. 21 Cheriss May/NurPhoto/Getty Images; p. 25 Featureflash Photo Agency/Shutterstock.com; p. 30 Ababsolutum/E+/Getty Images; p. 34 Efisko Aleksandr/Shutterstock.com photo is being used for illustrative purposes only, the person in the photo is a model); p. 36 Vasilisa Tsoy/Shutterstock.com; p. 38 Courtesy Abigail O'laughlin/Project HEAL; p. 45 Ian Boddy/Science Source; p. 51 ScreenShot; p. 54 Solovyova/iStockphoto.com; p. 56 BraunS/E+/Getty Images; p. 62 Tommaso Boddi/WireImage/Getty Images; p. 65 Designua/Shutterstock.com; p. 68 Eranicle/Shutterstock.com; p. 70 Alberto E. Rodriguez/Getty Images; p. 74 Wellcome Library, London. Wellcome Images/Wikimedia Commons/File:Richard Morton Wellcome L0060742.jpg/CC BY 4.0; p. 76 BSIP/Science Source; p. 80 Jupiter55/iStockphoto.com; p. 87 RJ Sangosti/The Denver Post/Getty Images; p. 90 Chinnapong/Shutterstock.com; p. 92 Thomas Niedermueller/Bongarts/Getty Images; p. 102 Lealnard Riengkaew/Shutterstock.com.

Printed in the United States of America

CONTENTS

Chapter 1

Understanding Eating Disorders

Half of all Americans have a sad fact in common: they know someone who has had an eating disorder. In the United States, thirty million people of all ages will experience an eating disorder themselves during their lives. This is a serious problem. Eating disorders rob people of their health and happiness. For some, they are fatal. Eating disorders are the number-one cause of death for females ages fifteen to twenty-four. Yet

Opposite: If you have an eating disorder, you do not have to suffer alone. Family doctors are a great resource for help and advice.

eating disorders remain largely misunderstood by the public and even by some medical professionals. There are also many dangerous myths about eating disorders. These false beliefs cause many people suffering from eating disorders, their family and friends, and sometimes their doctors to miss the early warning signs, misdiagnose the illness, and mistreat it. Despite new federal laws, treatment remains expensive, and it is often not covered by medical insurance. Research funding is low compared with how many people have an eating disorder. Even when a person with an eating disorder is willing to seek treatment and is able to access it, the path to recovery is not short and smooth. Eating disorders require three-part recovery: physical, psychological, and behavioral. A person's body, mind, and habits must get back to normal, with the help of doctors.

Despite these challenges, there is a lot of hope. Every patient has the potential to become healthy again. Some researchers have even found that up to two-thirds of people with eating disorders eventually re-create healthy relationships with food and their bodies. An eating disorder is not a life sentence.

EATING DISORDERS ARE MENTAL DISORDERS

Most people know about eating disorders by the names of the individual illnesses, such as anorexia, binge eating, and bulimia. However, an eating disorder is any change in eating that causes physical or mental harm. Eating too little (anorexia), eating too much (binge eating disorder), or forced vomiting (bulimia) are just a few examples of eating disorders. Someone with pica, which means repeatedly eating things that are not food, suffers from an eating disorder. So does someone with rumination disorder, which often involves regurgitating food and then rechewing or reswallowing it.

Eating disorders affect the body and physical health as well as mental and emotional health. Some disorders quickly attack nearly all organs and body systems. Nearly all co-occur, or happen at the same

Scales Are Not the True Measurement of the Problem

Eating disorders are not really about looks and weight. An obsession about food and body size is a key part of eating disorders, but it is never the full story. Focusing on physical appearance is not the reason for eating disorders, and stopping a fixation on looks is usually not the solution to them.

Studies have shown links between eating disorders and other obsessions, such as perfectionism in academics and sports. Many people report that they use eating disorder behaviors to deal with depression or anxiety. This becomes a vicious cycle. The coping technique (the eating disorder) that helps people with depression or anxiety feel better temporarily causes longer-lasting physical and mental harm. In turn, this intensifies the depression or anxiety, which leads the person to more disordered eating.

Some people with eating disorders never claim to feel unhappy with their weight or appearance. This is particularly common in younger children who develop eating disorders before they become teenagers. They are not trying to have a certain body shape. They are much more often trying to soften some other pain they feel.

Experts agree that getting a patient back to a healthy weight and to consuming nutritious food is only the first step in recovery from an eating disorder. A person is not cured simply because they are no longer focused on their body. Instead, getting physically healthy means a person can participate more meaningfully in emotional therapy. The work necessary to solve the mental issue underlying the eating disorder usually continues long after a healthy weight is reestablished.

time, with mental health conditions such as anxiety and depression. In fact, eating disorders themselves are considered mental illnesses.

People do not choose to have an eating disorder. They contract, or get, the disorder just as they do other diseases or conditions. Eating disorders are complex illnesses that involve many factors: genetics (meaning family history); biology (the makeup of each unique person); environment (for example, if the person had physical illnesses, was bullied, or had other stress); and social elements (like body ideals shown in media).

Even though we cannot see an eating disorder under a microscope or with an X-ray, doctors can recognize eating disorders in their patients. Medical professionals diagnose patients based on definitions in the American Psychiatric Association's *Diagnostic and Statistical Manual of Mental Disorders, Fifth Edition*. This reference book is known by its abbreviation, the DSM-5. It defines medically recognized mental health conditions, disorders, and illnesses. The DSM-5 groups symptoms together to classify distinct, individual eating disorders.

Anorexia Nervosa

Anorexia's full name is anorexia nervosa. It is the third–most common chronic illness for teenagers. It also has a high death rate. Teenagers with anorexia are much more likely to die by suicide than are people without anorexia. According to the DSM-5, people with anorexia have the following symptoms:

- They do not eat enough food to maintain a weight that is appropriate for their age and overall development and health.
- They are incredibly scared to gain weight.
- Their weight may be considered normal or even a little too heavy, but they have lost a lot of weight.
- They have an incorrect understanding of what they weigh and how they look. Even if they are underweight,

they think they weigh too much. They think they appear overweight, and they do not like that.

- They think their worth as a person is connected to how much they weigh and how they look to others.
- They do not think their decreasing weight and poor eating habits are unhealthy.

Anorexia is a common condition in the American fashion industry. Researchers and advocates have found that most models are asked to change their body size and shape in order to get or keep work. These unreasonable—and dangerous—expectations and demands have been happening for a long time. In 1974, Beverly Johnson became the first African American to be a cover model for *Vogue*. For this twenty-one-year-old, her career, her role in the community, and her self-worth were tied entirely to her weight and shape. She wrote in her 2015 memoir that if people she worked with liked the way she

In 1974, Beverly Johnson was a top model—and she was suffering from an eating disorder.

looked, that meant she as a person was "fabulous." So, Johnson said, she ate nothing. She and other models did not even drink water because they believed it would make them fat.

Decades later, singer Kesha experienced similar pressure. As a new star in her early twenties, she struggled with criticism and the pressure to excel. In response, she told *Vogue* in 2015, she "went to a dark place." Her brain shut off her interest in eating. She started to equate deep feelings of hunger with goodness, even though she did not feel great at all. That was because "the worse it got, the more positive feedback I was getting," Kesha explained. People gave her compliments on what they could see—her weight and shape—but they

Kesha starved herself in response to pressure to be a superstar entertainer.

could not see that she was sad and that the changes in her body were not healthy. She needed support and treatment, not praise.

Binge Eating Disorder

Binge eating disorder (BED) is the most common eating disorder, but understanding it can be confusing.

Bingeing—eating a lot of food in one sitting—is something many Americans do at one time or another. That does not mean most Americans have BED. Teammates play a tough soccer game and then celebrate the big win with lots of pizza. Families linger at the dinner table during a holiday meal and refill their plates way more than they would normally. Friends hang out together eating popcorn and ice cream while binge-watching TV. All of those are normal special occasions.

Doctors, therapists, and nurses follow the DSM-5 carefully to understand how BED differs from the infrequent splurge. The DSM-5 lists the specific symptoms for BED. These show how someone with that eating disorder behaves differently than someone who occasionally binge eats but is otherwise healthy:

- People with BED eat more food over a period of time than most people would eat in that same amount of time and under the same circumstances. That combination of factors is important.
- They feel out of control when they are overeating.
- They binge eat at least once a week for three months.
- They do not balance their overeating by exercising more than usual or by fasting between binges. They do not make themselves throw up after overeating.

In addition to the above, people with BED do at least three of these things each time they binge:

- Eat more quickly than usual
- Eat until they are so full it hurts
- Eat even when they are not hungry
- Eat alone because they feel embarrassed by what they are doing
- Feel negatively about themselves after bingeing

People with BED can be any weight, from what is considered medically normal to what doctors may call obese. Monica Seles is a retired professional tennis player who is also recovering from BED. As a teen, she was fit and weighed an amount considered normal for her age, height, and intense level of physical activity. When she was sixteen years old, she won her first Grand Slam title, the most important award in tennis. Suddenly, this young star athlete was under more pressure than ever before. She kept working out at a rate normal for her job as a tennis player, but she began eating much more than was normal. She kept her bingeing a secret from her friends, family, and coaches because she was embarrassed and ashamed that she was so disciplined on the tennis court but so out of control with food. Eventually, she admitted to herself that she was in trouble and needed help. She talked with her doctor, and together, they came up with a plan to adjust her eating—and her mindset. When she was in her forties and leading a healthy life once again, Seles began speaking publicly about her eating disorder and how much better she felt once she asked for help and did the work to get better.

Bulimia Nervosa

Bulimia nervosa is known by its shortened name, bulimia. Many people think of bulimia patients as people who make themselves throw up after eating. Throwing up is only one symptom of bulimia. According to the DSM-5, people are bulimic if they do the following:

- They binge eat, just like someone with BED does.
- Unlike people with BED, people with bulimia try to counteract their binges with inappropriate opposite actions. They may purge food from their systems. To do this, they may throw up. They may also take laxatives, which forces them to use the bathroom more than is normal. They also may exercise too much or not eat between binges.
- Like people with anorexia, people with bulimia equate their self-worth with their weight and shape. They are often of normal weight or a little overweight.

Actor Gabourey Sidibe, known for her first big role in the movie *Precious* and for her current long-running role on the television show *Empire*, lived with untreated depression for years. When she was in college, her depression took a scary turn. She wrote in her 2017 memoir that the way she dealt with her

Actor Gabourey Sidibe's depression led to bulimia.

saddest moments was to force herself to throw up—sometimes all she had ingested was a little bread and a little water, but she would still purge. When she did finally start therapy, she was diagnosed with bulimia. She had not been throwing up to lose weight—the truth was she had been purging to deal with her depression.

After years of working with a therapist and a nutritionist, Sidibe no longer feels like making herself purge. She is in a place of acceptance about her depression—and now that is what makes her feel good. Her depression is a part of her, but she has learned healthy tools that she can use to move herself through her dark periods.

A Young Life Makes a Difference

President Obama signs the 21st Century Cures Act.

On December 13, 2016, then-president Barack Obama made history by signing the 21st Century Cures Act (Cures Act) into law. This became the first US federal law to recognize eating disorders as a mental health issue.

The Anna Westin Act, part of the Cures Act, requires most health insurance companies to cover treatment for eating disorders just as they do for other mental health concerns. It also discusses educating doctors and nurses so they can recognize early warning signs of eating disorders in patients. The Anna Westin Act is named for a young woman from Minnesota. She suffered from anorexia for five years, and then she died by suicide in the year 2000 when she was twenty-one years old. At one point during her illness, she wrote in her diary, "I am scared … about what's going on right now. I can't have any control over my own mind. As much as I know what I need to do, it's so hard to."

The National Eating Disorders Association (NEDA), the Eating Disorders Coalition (EDC), the Emily Foundation, Anna Westin's family, and other groups advocated for eating disorders to be included in the Cures Act. The Anna Westin Act shows that eating disorder advocacy groups make a real difference. These groups work hard to make sure that everyone has access to lifesaving treatment.

Other Specified Feeding or Eating Disorders

Medical professionals also recognize mental illness in people who are seriously suffering but who do not have all the symptoms of an eating disorder. The DSM-5 calls these conditions "other specified feeding or eating disorders" (OSFED).

For example, if someone had all the symptoms of BED but binge ate every other week instead of once a week, that person technically would not meet the DSM-5 definition of a BED patient. However, that person could still be quite sick. A doctor may diagnose that person as having "binge eating disorder of low frequency and/or limited duration." Another example of other specified eating disorders is night eating syndrome. A person with that illness does not have all the symptoms of a binge eater but does eat too much after dinner or in the middle of the night.

Orthorexia nervosa is another mental health condition that is not recognized by the DSM-5, but medical professionals are concerned about it. Doctors started recognizing the condition in the late 1990s. The name means "fixation on righteous eating." It is good to eat nutritious foods, but an extreme obsession on "safe" foods versus "unsafe" foods can be unhealthy. People with orthorexia may do the following:

- They may spend hours each day thinking about food, planning meals, and reading nutrition labels. It is smart to pay attention to what you eat, but it is excessive to let that be the only thing you think about.
- They may refuse to eat whole categories of food, like all foods that include dairy or all foods that have preservatives. They are not doing this because they are genuinely allergic to an ingredient or because they do not like the taste; they are doing this because they have decided, without facts, that that food is not safe for them to eat.

- They are scared to eat even one dish or meal that they did not prepare or that falls out of their specifications.
- They judge their friends and family for eating foods in that "unsafe" category.
- As with diagnosed eating disorders, people with orthorexia feel guilt and shame about their obsession.

Experts do not know if orthorexia should be considered a full, independent eating disorder, or part of an existing eating disorder, or part of a different mental illness. Regardless, people suffering from orthorexia require treatment. Because orthorexia has similarities with both anorexia and obsessive compulsive disorder, many medical professionals suggest treatment similar to what is recommended for those conditions.

Pop star Zayn Malik has written about his undiagnosed eating disorder. He suffers from anxiety, and restricting his eating was his way to control what felt like an out-of-control mental state. Looking back on his years with the group One Direction when he was a teenager, he wrote in his 2018 memoir, "It wasn't as though I had any concerns about my weight or anything like that, I'd just go for days—sometimes two or three days straight—without eating anything at all. It got quite serious."

Singer Zayn Malik has opened up about his undiagnosed eating disorder.

IS THE MEDIA TO BLAME?

One of the biggest false assumptions about eating disorders is that the media is responsible for them. Websites, videos, television, movies, magazines, social media, and the celebrities that make their livings in media can't "give" someone an eating disorder.

Remember, having an eating disorder is not a choice. No one who admires a model's Instagram selfies or wishes they looked like their favorite television actor or athlete can make themselves have an eating disorder. They can choose to go on a diet to try to look like that celebrity, but that alone will not start a disorder. Only those people with a certain mental and physical biology, along with living in a certain environment, will be triggered by that first diet—they may then get an eating disorder. Therefore, the media helps to create a culture that supports the existence of eating disorders, but it is not wholly responsible for them.

The Effect of the Media on People's Beliefs and Behaviors

The media influences how people want to look, and that can start some people on the path to developing an eating disorder. Studies have shown that people in magazines and television shows as well as fashion models have gotten thinner since the 1950s. At the same time, people in the United States and Canada have gotten heavier. Also at the same time, there has been a big increase in ads and commercials for diet foods and other products to help people lose weight. This means there is a growing gap between the ideal body, as defined by the media, and the actual body size of most people. Because the media offers ways to narrow that gap (through advertisements for diet products), there is also a clear emphasis on the importance of body size.

Other studies have shown this affects people's perspective and expectations for their own bodies. Magazines aimed at girls and women contain more than ten times as many weight-loss ads as magazines aimed at boys and men. When asked how they would like to change their lives, most girls and women report they wish to change their weight. This desire is so common that therapists created the term "normative discontent" to describe it. Normative discontent means that it is normal for females to feel unhappy about their weight.

One study, set in the tiny South Pacific island nation of Fiji, is considered a clear example of the media's role in people's expectations about weight. It can be difficult to prove the media's influence in a country as big as the United States, where so much of the world's media has come for decades. Not so in Fiji.

Western television was not broadcast there until 1995, so researchers had the opportunity to study teen girls both before Western influence and after. Also, the traditional Fijian culture values different beauty markers than Western media has. Where Western media celebrates thinness and dieting, Fijian culture is almost the exact opposite. It celebrates curvy bodies and eating regular meals. The researchers wondered if Fijians' perspective would change to agree with what Western media told them. They found it did.

In 1995, almost no teen girls in Fiji reported dieting to lose weight, and none said they purged.

Within three years, the majority of teen girls, 74 percent, said they felt they were too fat. Nearly all of them tried to address that with diets. More than 11 percent were purging. Girls who lived in a house with television—and even those who did not but who had friends who did—were more likely to experience disordered eating.

DIVERSE CONDITIONS WITH A COMMON SOLUTION

Eating disorders are diverse—the symptoms range from eating too little to eating too much—as are the people who suffer from them and the reasons they get the disorder. These disorders share one thing in common: they are all mental illnesses, so nobody is at fault for developing one, and everyone should seek treatment.

Chapter 2

The Risks of Eating Disorders

The short answer to the question "Who is at risk of developing an eating disorder?" is "anyone." Eating disorders are not connected to the color of a person's skin, their gender, their age, how much money their family has, how much they weigh, or any other factor. Just like all other mental illnesses, and many physical illnesses, eating disorders can affect anyone at any time in life. No one can predict with 100 percent accuracy every person who will

Opposite: Eating disorders can affect anyone. Be there for your friends and classmates.

develop an eating disorder. However, experts have named many of the factors that put an individual at greater risk to experience an eating disorder.

Age is one risk factor for eating disorders, which are most common in teenagers and young adults. Another risk factor is gender. Girls and young women are most likely to be diagnosed and treated for eating disorders. Very little research has been done on eating disorders in transgender populations. However, the few existing studies show that young people who identify as transgender are at much greater risk of having anorexia or bulimia than are their cisgender peers.

Sexual orientation could also be a risk factor. While teenage girls and young women who identify as lesbian and those who identify as straight are equally as likely to develop eating disorders, the rate of eating disorders in gay teenage boys and young men is slightly higher than it is in straight male teens and young men. However, it's impossible to know if that is the whole story, or if gay teens and young men appear more vulnerable simply because they report the problem and seek treatment more.

On the other hand, research shows that family history affects the likelihood of developing an eating disorder. A person with a parent or a sibling with an eating disorder is more at risk of also developing one. Participation in certain activities might also play a role. Gymnasts, runners, wrestlers, and dancers may experience eating disorders more than teens in other activities.

Finally, environment is a factor. People who believe media images and articles that promote certain body sizes and shapes; who face peer pressure to look a certain way; who have been bullied or abused; and/or who are going through major changes like starting college or a job or preparing for a big event are more likely to have an eating disorder.

MENTAL HEALTH RISK FACTORS

The brain offers more clues to who is at risk of developing an eating disorder. Remember, above

A person with an eating disorder has a distorted perspective about their body's shape and size.

all else, eating disorders are mental illnesses. Even though eating disorders may seem to develop in people who look a certain way, the actual key to what is happening is in a person's head.

Body Dysmorphic Disorder

Eating disorders are often coping mechanisms for other mental illnesses, such as anxiety, depression, and impulsive behavior. People with body dysmorphic disorder (BDD) are particularly vulnerable to eating disorders. People with BDD have a nearly constant focus on an imagined or slight defect in their appearance. Worrying that they have a huge imperfection overrides all other thoughts most of the time.

BDD affects females and males almost equally. Muscle dysmorphia is a common manifestation of BDD in males. A person with that obsession is extremely concerned about being strong and having big muscles. BDD usually starts when a person is around twelve or thirteen years old. People with BDD will do whatever they can to improve what they think is wrong about their bodies—including developing eating disorders.

Different Circuitry

There is new research that suggests that people with eating disorders have brains that are wired differently than other people's brains. This would help to explain why not everyone unhappy with their weight, stressed about school, or young and female develops an eating disorder. "Culture plays some role—but maybe less so than we thought in the past," said Walter Kaye. Kaye is the director of the Eating Disorders Treatment and Research Program at the University of California, San Diego School of Medicine. He is also one of the researchers leading the way to understand the connection between the brain and eating disorders.

Work by researchers across the United States has shown that people with anorexia can ignore the feeling of being hungry. Their brains care

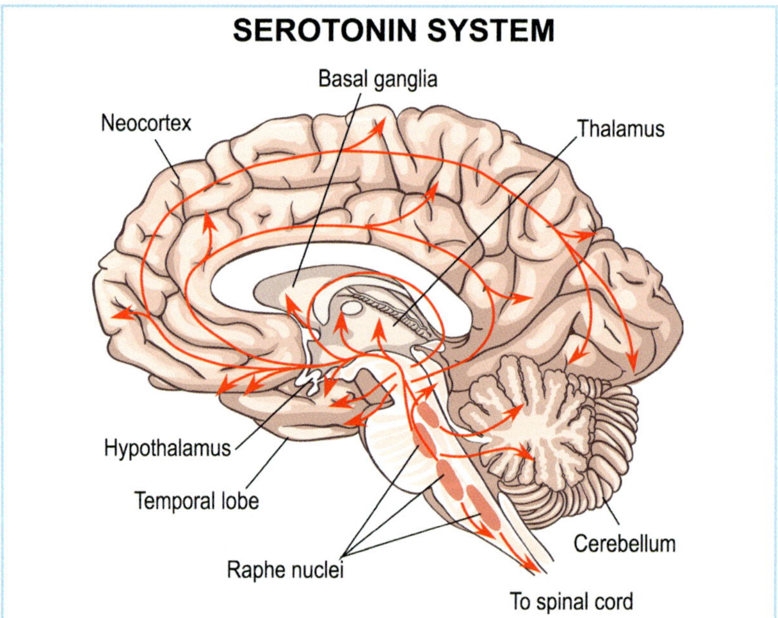

Researchers think the brain's serotonin system plays a role in eating disorders developing.

less about getting a reward when they are hungry than other people's brains do. Their brains do not release the same amount of chemical messages that healthy brains release, which tell the body to desire a reward of food. This is crystal clear in studies that do not involve food. The brains of people with anorexia behave differently all the time. Kaye and his colleagues watched the brain activity of women with and without anorexia while the women placed bets in a game. The brains of the women with anorexia were less active when the women won and more active when they lost.

The same is true for people with bulimia. The part of the brain that tells a person that food is tasty to eat and good for the body is weaker than normal. People with bulimia also have less serotonin, a neurotransmitter that helps people feel relaxed and happy (and hungry), which might be why negative responses, like anxiety, can overtake them.

Basically, the brains of people who develop eating disorders may be wired to help them starve

HEALing Together

Liana Rosenman and Kristina Saffran were two teenagers who survived their own eating disorders— and went on to help others recover from their struggles with eating. When they were fifteen years old, they founded Project HEAL, which stands for Help to: Eat, Accept, and Live.

Rosenman was in seventh grade when she went on her first diet, which spiraled into an addiction to watching the scale. It took her years to beat this addiction, which her doctor diagnosed as anorexia, and it nearly killed her when she was in high school.

Liana Rosenman (*left*) and Kristina Saffran (*right*) founded Project HEAL when they were fifteen.

Saffran was diagnosed with anorexia when she was ten years old. Like Rosenman, she became obsessed with weighing herself. Three different times when she was thirteen years old, she lied to her parents and took the city bus to the store to buy new scales.

The two met in 2006 when they were both thirteen and in treatment at the same facility. They discovered similar beginnings to their illnesses: Rosenman cited her perfectionism and desire for constant success as key pieces to the puzzle that forms her disorder. Saffran said her first diet was not about losing weight but about setting a goal and achieving it quickly. Two years later, they were both in recovery and feeding their focus in new, positive ways. Project HEAL began as a fundraising organization for people trying to pay for treatment. In 2017, Project HEAL began offering early intervention and recovery support in addition to financial aid. In 2011, when Rosenman and Saffran were eighteen years old, *Glamour* magazine awarded them Women of the Year awards for their work.

themselves or binge eat. The longer the disease goes untreated, the more brains will adapt and tell the body that the diseased state of living is normal.

DIGGING DEEPER

Just as some groups of people are considered more at risk of developing eating disorders, other groups are believed to be less vulnerable to them. For example, if teenage girls and young women are more likely to develop eating disorders, then it seems logical to say that teenage boys and young men are less likely. That assumption is not always correct. Often this confusion is the result of too little information. Researchers do not have a lot of data about the rate of eating disorders in some groups. That means people can think there is no problem when, in reality, we simply do not know whether or not there is an issue. There is also complex information about some groups, which means there is no easy answer about their eating disorder risk. Experts must look closely to understand how eating disorders truly affect them. Stopping at the thought, "A person from this group is more likely to suffer from eating disorders than a person from that group," misses what is truly going on.

Racial Reasons for Underreporting

When it comes to race and eating disorders, the available data is both limited and complex. Eating disorders affect people of all races and cultures. That is about the only thing experts can say for certain on this topic. It is not really known if one group suffers more than another because researchers have not studied all groups equally.

For example, a lot is known about white people and eating disorders because researchers have studied white people and eating disorders a lot. There was not much study of Native Americans and eating disorders until about 2011. Because of that, experts know little about rates and types of eating disorders among the indigenous populations of the United States. That does not mean no connection exists.

Many people of different racial groups have concerns about going to the doctor because of discrimination. The Urban Health Media Project, a joint program of Howard University and Morgan State University, found that parents can become concerned that their parenting skills and choices will be judged and their children maybe even taken away from them. They are concerned about "telling secrets" to people outside their community. This fear of reporting means experts do not accurately know how eating disorders affect certain groups, and patients do not get the treatment they need.

People may also underreport because of perceived pressures from their communities. People from groups who have experienced great hardship—such as African Americans, who survived slavery and fought for civil rights—may think their problems with eating disorders are minor in comparison and not ask their friends and family for help. Stephanie Covington Armstrong, who wrote the book *Not All Black Girls Know How to Eat: A Story of Bulimia*, has said of her eating disorder, "I needed to suffer in silence, that somehow my legacy of strong, independent ancestors did not allow me to lean on anyone outside my community."

Others may feel pulled in two different directions by their cultures. Rosie Molinary understands this well. She is a Latina American author and activist specializing in issues of body image and self-acceptance. Her book *Hijas Americanas: Beauty, Body Image, and Growing Up Latina* is about the pressure to conform to the standards of beauty of both Latin culture and dominant US culture. These two definitions of the ideal body are historically quite different from each other, so Latinx people may feel they fail to be beautiful in one or both of their cultures. They feel as if they are always about to be judged, Molinary has said. If a person in this group has an eating disorder, it may be hard for them to recognize it or feel comfortable enough to tell someone about it.

Eating Disorders Are Not "Female Diseases"

Eating disorders among males are not well understood either. Many people have wrongly considered eating disorders "female diseases" that survive because of social pressures on women about their weight. This discourages some boys and men from seeking proper diagnosis and treatment for eating disorders.

In turn, this means that estimates about how many males are affected are likely inaccurate. The National Alliance on Mental Illness estimates that at least 10 percent of Americans with eating disorders are male. The National Association for Males with Eating Disorders estimates 25 percent to 40 percent of people with eating disorders are boys or men. The Centers for Disease Control and Prevention have estimated up to 33 percent of people with eating disorders are male. Each expert organization offers its own best guess. Because of gender-based myths around eating disorders, even the experts are uncertain.

PAYING ATTENTION IS THE FIRST STEP

If you or someone you know might be experiencing the beginnings of an eating disorder, it is time for you to start conducting your own research. Pay attention to thoughts, behaviors, and triggers and stressors. You are searching for an understanding of what happens and when. You are noticing patterns of negative thoughts and dangerous behaviors. Ask questions of yourself or the person you know who might be in trouble.

People with eating disorders often obsessively weigh themselves.

Only medical professionals such as doctors and therapists can diagnose a person with an eating disorder. You are observing and gathering as much detailed information as you can because that will help you know if there is something going on that a doctor should know about. If there is a problem, the information you now know will help the doctor make an accurate diagnosis.

Questions to Ask

Think back over the past month. Consider whether you never did the following things, did them always or a lot, or did them somewhere in between, like often, sometimes, or rarely.

- How many times did you have negative thoughts or feelings about your body?
- How many times did you feel bad about eating?
- How many times did you put restrictions on your eating? How many times did you ignore all guidelines around eating? For example, how many times did you make yourself eat less than you normally would?

How many times did you find yourself eating more than you normally would? Did you change what types of foods you ate?

- How many times did you vomit?
- How many times did you use substances to control your weight? These could be prescription medication or over-the-counter medication or some other type of substance.
- How many times did you exercise with the goal of changing your body size or shape?
- How many times did your thoughts or behaviors around eating or your body prevent you from doing other things you needed or wanted to do?
- How many times have your friends and family been worried about your weight, eating, or exercising?
- How many times were you secretive about your feelings or behaviors around your body and your weight?

It is good to ask yourself these questions because they help you understand what you are experiencing, but also remember that you are never alone. Use these answers to help you talk with a trusted adult about what you are going through and what help you need.

Questions to Ask Yourself About a Loved One

You can also ask these types of questions about a friend, sibling, or other relative you are worried about. Think back over the past month. Consider whether that person never did the following things, did them always or a lot, or did them somewhere in between, like often, sometimes, or rarely.

- Have you noticed strange behaviors around food? Does your friend suddenly hide food? Only eat certain foods? Combine types of food in unusual ways?

- Does your friend overeat or undereat?
- Does your friend always or often hurry to the bathroom immediately after eating?
- Has your friend started taking something to try to help control weight, like diet pills?
- Is your friend exercising more than usual?
- Has your friend lost or gained a lot of weight?
- Do you know if mealtimes are stressful at home or at school for your friend?
- Do you think your friend is keeping secrets from their family about eating and exercising?
- Have you noticed that person seeming sad, worried, or guilty about what they are eating or how their body looks?

Social Media and Eating Disorders

The media can play a role in the development of eating disorders, so social media can as well. Magazines, television, and movies show thin models and actors and advertise weight-loss products. Social media connects people directly with these celebrities. They seem like friends we can trust. Sometimes they publish posts that look like personal messages, but they are actually ads for diet and exercise products and programs that celebrities are paid to share. These are called spon con, short for sponsored content. Spon con's celebration of one body size may start to feel like pressure for you to have that one body size too.

Cyberbullying is also an aspect of social media—and a contributor to eating disorders. Body-shaming is one of the most common forms of bullying online. The media often tells people that muscular, thin bodies are the ideal, and it is easy for cyberbullies to latch on to that ideal and terrorize people who do not meet that

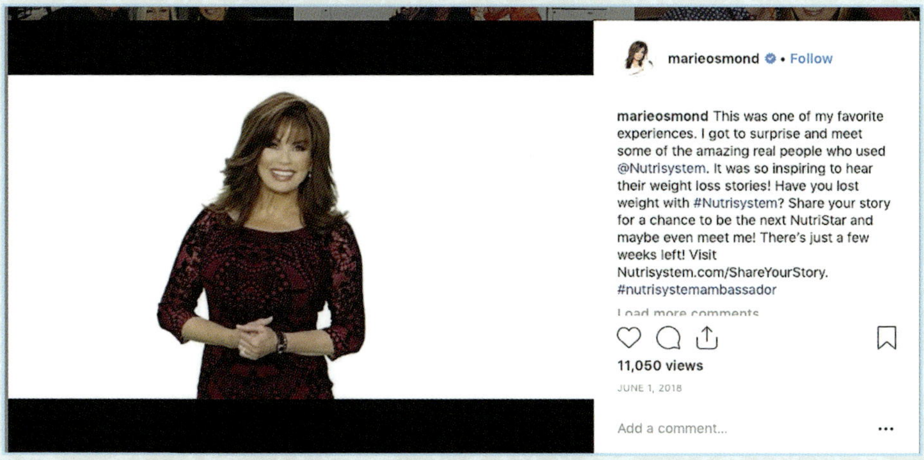

Celebrities often endorse diet products on social media.

standard. These bullies may be classmates, or they may be complete strangers. Some online forums run entire discussion threads with the goal of body-shaming people publicly. Sixty-five percent of people with eating disorders say bullying fueled their eating disorder. If you experience cyberbullying, do not respond to the messages. Instead, turn to a trusted adult like a parent or teacher right away. They can help you block the cyberbully, record all the important information about what happened, and report the messages to authorities. You are not to blame; it is important you tell an adult what happened.

Thinking about what you have been noticing is helpful, but it is not a diagnosis. Only a medical professional can determine if your friend or relative has an eating disorder. And it is up to that person to go to a doctor. It can be difficult talking with them about what you observe—and doing so is not your responsibility alone. Talk to an adult you trust, and that person will help with taking the next steps.

PREVENT EATING DISORDERS BEFORE THEY BEGIN

There are ways to stop an eating disorder before it begins. Keep track of your ideas about food and body image. Communicate honestly if you find yourself starting to struggle. There are other good prevention ideas too.

First, find out what resources are available to you. Does your school have a mental health counselor? Are there support groups for teens and young adults in your community? Of course, if you have not been talking with them already, do not forget your parents and other trusted adults. If you are nervous about talking with them, ask a counselor for ideas on how to start.

Next, keep busy in positive ways. The Born This Way Foundation, which was founded by singer, actor, and advocate Lady Gaga, conducted a survey in 2017 on mental health in young people. The teens and young adults who answered the questions named their top ways to feel better mentally and emotionally. These included exercising, doing a creative activity, hanging out with friends, following a religious or spiritual practice, doing yoga, and following along with mindfulness apps.

Finally, eat meals with your family as often as you can. Tons of research shows this simple act can have major benefits. When families eat together at least three times a week, teen food and body health skyrockets: teens are 35 percent less likely to develop an eating disorder, 24 percent more likely to eat

Eating meals with others can help encourage healthy habits.

nutritious food, and 12 percent less likely to be overweight. Ask your parents if you can help plan and prepare the meals, so your favorites get on the menu too.

The reason early detection and prevention of eating disorders is important is because eating disorders are extremely dangerous. They harm all parts of the body and brain and can have lasting physical, mental, and emotional consequences. While it's never too late to seek help, stopping eating disorders before they start can save you or someone you love a lot of pain.

Chapter 3

Experiencing Eating Disorders

"Mental health is the chronic illness of the young," Ken Duckworth, medical director for the National Alliance on Mental Illness, has said. Three-quarters of mental health issues begin before age twenty-five, half by age fifteen. This is why eating disorders, which are mental health disorders, often begin when people are young.

AN ILLUSION OF CONTROL

For a teenager, life can feel out of control. Every day, adults at home, at school, in activities, and at work

Opposite: Teens' lives are full of pressure. Eating disorders can seem to offer a sense of control, but it's a false sense of control.

direct what teens do and when they do it. There are many things that teens are not in charge of, yet they are held responsible for completing important tasks and making life-altering decisions, all while balancing new experiences like dating. The self-imposed structure of eating disorders can give teens the illusion of control within all that chaos.

Pooja Patel was entering her teenage years when she found the control she was craving in an eating disorder. In an interview, she said, "A way that I could control all of those outside things was by controlling my body." She did not choose to get sick, but when she was, she felt a sort of peace in being the only one in charge of her diet and weight. This was, of course, a false peace, and a false control, as she would find out. However, in the moment, she believed it was true.

Shayna Gonzalvez developed an eating disorder when she was eleven or twelve. She explained: "When I'm feeling most stressed about something, I become very, very precise about what I eat because it's almost like I need to somehow take control of my body when I feel like everything else is falling apart."

Because eating disorders are mental health disorders, all of them—from anorexia to binge eating disorder (BED) to bulimia—are tied to psychological issues. Depression, anxiety, substance use, obsessive compulsive disorder, and other conditions often contribute to the start of an eating disorder. People who have eating disorders or who are vulnerable to suffering from them experience some kind of calm or release related to their food habits. For example, a person with a healthy relationship to food will be cranky or experience some other negative response when they start to diet, even if they are doing so sensibly and for good reason. Their body is no longer getting all that it is used to receiving. That restriction or denial causes an automatic response that makes dieting feel difficult. However, a person who has or who is vulnerable to developing anorexia feels calm or has other positive reactions when they begin a diet. This is why a person with an eating disorder often also suffers from depression or anxiety or obsessive compulsive disorder (OCD). Controlling their food intake and body size and shape feels to them as much like a calming drug as prescription medication or alcohol or drugs feel to others.

Of course, this calm is just an illusion. People with eating disorders are not truly in control.

Eating disorders also change the mind and the body completely. Even if a person with a disorder felt in control of their actions, they would not be able to control the havoc those actions would create inside them.

Psychological issues grow and manifest as the eating disorder continues. Eating disorders make people behave strangely around food and exercise and think abnormally about their bodies. This can lead to guilt, shame, and feelings of inadequacy, which can intensify anxiety and depression.

Physically, eating disorders do not affect only a person's weight. Experts encourage teens to start treatment long before body changes are noticeable. The dangers associated with eating disorders start early, can do serious damage, and can last a long time. The sooner the eating disorder is treated, the more likely its effects can be reversed.

THE DEADLY CONSEQUENCES OF ANOREXIA

Anorexia hurts nearly every system in the body. This makes it the deadliest mental health disorder. The longer a person has it, the more likely that person will die from it—in fact, as many as 20 percent of people with anorexia will die. Some of these deaths are from suicide—females with anorexia are fifty-seven times more likely to die by suicide than other women are. Many of these deaths occur because anorexia is so damaging to the body that the body shuts itself down. The two longest-lasting or most serious physical issues that anorexia causes are heart and bone damage.

Slaying the Dragon

Actor Troian Bellisario speaks in support of other young people with eating disorders.

Troian Bellisario is known for her starring role in the television show *Pretty Little Liars*. She has also been outspoken about her experience with an eating disorder. Bellisario began self-harming when she was a junior in high school. She did so not to change her body but in response to school stress and anxiety. She would not allow herself to eat or go out with friends if she did not think she had done well in school that day. She was diagnosed with anorexia and eventually went through a lot of therapy.

Bellisario wrote and starred in a movie called *Feed* that is based on these experiences. Making a movie about her eating disorder was itself "like engaging with an addiction," she told *Interview* magazine; "It was like poking a sleeping dragon." Bellisario explored this feeling in the movie. *Feed* shows that once a person has an eating disorder, that relationship never fully disappears, even after treatment and recovery.

Because Bellisario acquired the tools to fight her eating disorder, she felt "empowered" to respond to that monster in a stronger way than she could have when she was in high school. "It's amazing," she said, "that you can have this huge, life-threatening thing be a part of you and still live inside of you, and almost tame it in a weird way."

Damage to the Heart

The heart needs certain electrolytes like potassium and calcium to work properly. They produce the electrical currents needed for the heart to beat normally. These electrolytes normally come into the body via the food a person eats. They dissolve in the body's fluids and flow to the heart.

People with anorexia do not eat a normal amount of nutrients, so there are fewer electrolytes available to the heart. A starved body is also a dehydrated body, which means there is also less fluid in the body to transport whatever potassium and calcium does exist.

Under these poor conditions, the heart pumps slower. The flow of blood reduces, and the blood pressure drops. The heart grows weaker. It even shrinks in size. Heart issues are the most common reason people with anorexia are admitted to the hospital.

Karen Carpenter is one of the most famous young people who had anorexia and also suffered from a heart condition. Her story introduced the public to anorexia. Before her, most people did not know what the disease was or that it even existed.

Carpenter and her brother were one of the most successful pop music acts of the 1970s, performing as the duo the Carpenters. Photos from 1970, when they had their first hit song, show her looking healthy. Five years later, the Carpenters were canceling tours because she was so sick. For less than eight years, she battled anorexia. Then, in early 1983, when she was only thirty-two years old, Carpenter died of a heart attack. It was caused by the physical strain on her heart from anorexia.

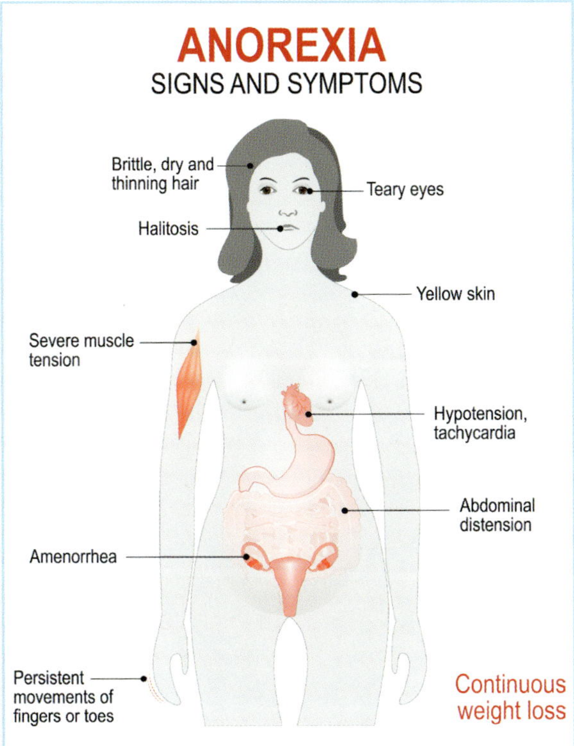

Anorexia has negative effects all over the body.

Damage to Bones

The medical term for having less bone density than is healthy is osteopenia. Osteoporosis is the same condition, but worse. Bones affected by these conditions can fracture or break easily. They also cannot hold a person up well, so that person begins to hunch over. Bones with low density can cause a person tremendous ongoing pain.

Those conditions have been considered problems of the old, and of women in particular. Bones grow stronger only until about age thirty. After that, they grow weaker, first slowly and then more rapidly.

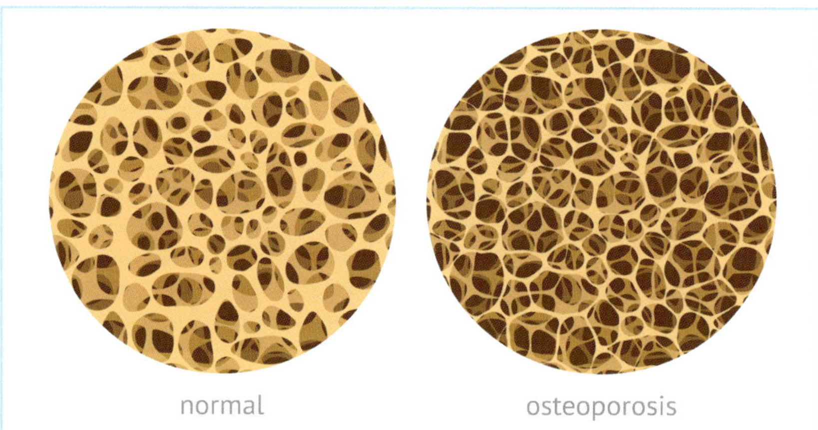

Anorexia can damage bones, making them less dense and then more vulnerable to breaking.

However, being anorexic can put even a young person at risk of developing osteopenia and maybe even osteoporosis.

As much as one-third of peak bone density happens during puberty—the same time anorexia often presents itself. If a person weighs too little, their body may stop producing hormones needed to build bone density. This problem can start as soon as six months after anorexia begins. Anorexia works fast at damaging bones.

Amenorrhea

Teen girls and young women who are anorexic can stop having their menstrual period or never start it. This has long-term effects for both their fertility later in life and their bone health. Low body weight can cause the female body to produce extra cortisol. This stress hormone reduces the amount of other hormones in the body. Without a sufficient amount of estrogen, for example, the body cannot regulate a monthly menstrual cycle.

A person who should have periods but does not has a condition called amenorrhea. This term is used whenever a period is missing, so even healthy people who are experiencing normal pregnancies have amenorrhea. However, missing a period each and every month for other reasons usually means there is a problem.

Menstruation that has stopped because of anorexia's toll on the body poses a big concern. If the anorexia remains untreated, the amenorrhea may continue. A chronically missing period will contribute to permanent bone loss. It also, more obviously, has an effect on fertility. As a person with amenorrhea gets older, becomes an independent adult, and wants to have children, that person will not be able to become pregnant.

Neurological Damage

Brain scans of people experiencing anorexia show that the brain physically changes when the disorder is active. The parts of the brain used for making smart decisions actually shrink. Because of this, and because of the lack of food fueling the brain, people with anorexia may not be able to think as well as they could before the disease. Some may also experience seizures or peripheral neuropathy—numbness or pain in the hands and feet. It happens because the peripheral nervous system, which carries messages from the brain to the rest of the body, has been damaged.

More Health Consequences

In addition to being at risk for these serious issues, people with anorexia face body changes that are not usually life threatening but that are problems nonetheless. These include:

- Experiencing anemia, or low red-blood-cell counts, or having low white-blood-cell counts. A person with a low blood-cell count of any kind has a weakened immune system. They become more vulnerable to all diseases and infections.

- Having hair and nails that break easily
- Having dry and yellowish skin
- Being constipated, or feeling like you have to use the restroom but being unable to
- Feeling cold all the time
- Feeling tired all the time

Nikki DuBose, a former model and now mental health advocate, started binge eating and purging when she was eight years old. When she developed anorexia in her twenties, her hair started falling out. Every time she showered, clumps easily slid out between her fingers. Because she lost so much, she

Nikki DuBose was a model who faced eating disorders. She now advocates for mental health.

eventually had to cut it short. Suddenly, when she looked in the mirror, she could barely recognize herself, and that made her want to react even more strongly and rip all her hair out. She eventually got treatment for her illness. Part of what she needed to do to be healthy was stop working in the fashion industry. She launched a new career—working to reduce eating disorders and offer support to people suffering trauma and mental illness. In 2016, she worked with NEDA and California Assemblyman Marc Levine on legislation that would require health and safety standards for models.

THE CONSEQUENCES OF BINGE EATING DISORDER

People with binge eating disorder (BED) are at risk of the same health concerns that people who are both obese and not physically active have. Ankles, knees, and hips can begin to hurt, if they have to support extra weight. The heart may struggle to pump effectively. Being overweight is the number one reason a person could contract type 2 diabetes, which damages organs and nerves.

It does not matter if a person with BED is not medically obese; because they consume large portions of food quickly, their bodies may be under a similar strain. Eating a lot of food in one sitting or eating late at night—two things BED sufferers do or may do often—are causes of gastroesophageal reflux disease (GERD). GERD is caused by stomach acid backwashing into the esophagus, the tube connecting the stomach and the mouth. It is the chronic and more serious version of heartburn.

Heartburn is the burning feeling between the breastbone and stomach that you may have experienced when after eating, for example, a big spicy meal right before going to bed. Experiencing that infrequently is uncomfortable but within the normal range of physical sensation. If a person feels at least that level of pain at least twice a week, that person may have GERD. The stomach acid backwash can wear away the soft-tissue lining of the esophagus, leaving sores that can bleed. If it is repeatedly damaged over time, the esophagus will develop scar tissue. This narrows the tube, making it harder to swallow because there is less room for food to fit.

THE CONSEQUENCES OF BULIMIA

Whether a person purges by abusing laxatives or by vomiting, bulimia is dangerous. As with anorexia, it is important to treat bulimia even before weight loss becomes apparent. This is for two main reasons. First, bulimia's side effects happen early in the disease, so it is important to address them before they get too bad and the damage done cannot easily be reversed. Also, people with bulimia do not always lose weight quickly. They can look exactly the same but be engaging in behaviors that harm their bodies.

A Centuries-Old Disease

Many people think eating disorders are modern mental illnesses. This is incorrect. The earliest known records of an eating disorder were not in the 2000s or even the 1900s. Richard Morton, a British doctor, wrote about anorexia in all the way back in 1689.

Richard Morton made the first known diagnosis of an eating disorder.

In his book, *Pthsiologia*, he did not call it anorexia, but the symptoms he described match doctors' understanding of the disease today. He called it "nervous consumption." *Pthsiologia* was about many consumptive, or wasting, diseases. One symptom of these diseases was losing weight or wasting away. Some of these diseases still exist, like tuberculosis (TB). We no longer categorize eating disorders as consumptive disorders, but it would have been logical for seventeenth-century doctors to do so. These diseases were serious in the 1600s because there was no treatment for them, and people usually died from them. Since Morton included anorexia in his book, he must have considered it very serious.

Morton wrote about anorexia in an eighteen-year-old girl and a sixteen-year-old boy. The girl "wholly neglected the care of herself for two full Years," Morton wrote. Denying that a situation is serious is one of the signs of anorexia. The boy, Morton wrote, "fell gradually into a total Want of Appetite, occasioned by his studying too hard." People with eating disorders often obsess about their school, work, and hobbies.

Laxative Abuse

People with bulimia who purge by forcing themselves to go to the bathroom a lot will not lose weight. According to Eating Disorder Hope, a resource center for people with eating disorders, "Taking laxatives for weight loss is like trying to drain a cup of water while someone is filling it up." In other words, it is a hopeless action. By the time the drug finally goes to work in the body, calories from eating have already been absorbed. People think laxatives work to lower weight because they feel lighter after using the bathroom, but as soon as they do something as minor as drink water, that "empty" feeling disappears. The person takes another laxative to feel thin again, and the process starts all over.

Taking laxatives a lot does not help a person lose weight, but it does cause a lot of damage to the body. Laxatives dehydrate the body and strip it of minerals and electrolytes. This can lead to the body's organs shutting down. The colon, the part of the large intestine that processes waste so it can be moved out of the body, becomes dependent on laxatives. It will not work without them. Laxative abuse can cause both constipation and chronic diarrhea. Colon cancer becomes a risk.

Vomiting

Vomiting to purge also severely damages the body. When a person throws up, it is not just food that comes up from the stomach. Naturally occurring acid, which helps the body digest food, also comes up. As it travels from the stomach to the mouth, it washes over the entire digestive tract, or path. This can lead to disorders such as esophagitis. That is an inflammation, or irritated swelling, of the esophagus, the

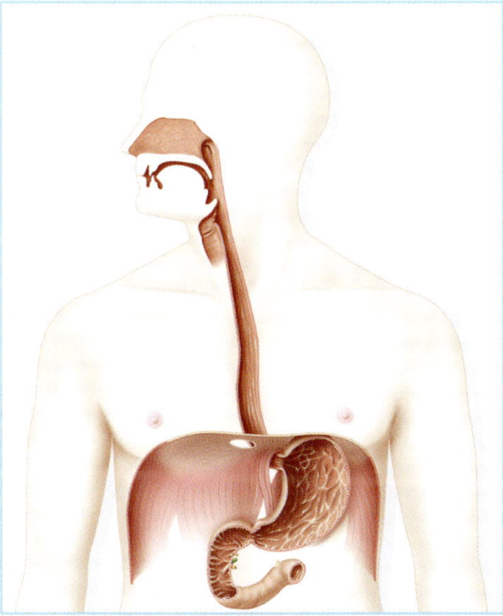

Because the stomach and the mouth are directly connected, purging can bring damaging stomach acid up into the throat and mouth.

muscular tube along which food and drink travels from the mouth to the stomach. Common symptoms include pain when swallowing and having a difficult time swallowing, food getting stuck in the esophagus, and even chest pain during eating.

When a person throws up, stomach acid also gets in the mouth and can damage teeth. Acid is corrosive, and it is strong enough to eat away the enamel that protects teeth. Losing this cover makes teeth sensitive. A person with bulimia may think they can enjoy eating food without gaining weight, but purging has made their teeth so sensitive that they can no longer enjoy things like having a soda with friends or going out for ice cream with their family.

Teeth without enamel are left vulnerable to developing cavities or chipping. They may turn yellow, no matter how hard a person brushes. In fact, brushing too much after each purge can also damage teeth.

Throwing up a lot can irritate the glands in the cheeks that produce saliva. Having a dry mouth is not just uncomfortable. It also means teeth are less protected because saliva helps prevent tooth decay.

Stomach acid is rough enough to damage teeth, so it is strong enough to hurt the tender skin along the roof and sides of the mouth and throat. The painful sores that develop can leave a person feeling like they always have a sore throat.

The terrible news is that eating disorders have devastating physical, mental, and emotional consequences. The incredible news is that they are treatable. The sooner medical attention begins, the likelier the consequences can also be reversed or at least successfully lessened. For every disorder and every consequence, there are medical options a teen can explore.

Chapter 4

Hope and Recovery

Eating disorders are treatable. However, that does not mean there is always a clear path to recovery. An eating disorder can appear when a person is a teenager and last through young adulthood. The disorder may then seem to disappear when the person is in their late twenties, thirties, and forties. When the person is in their fifties, the disorder may reappear. Or people may experience different eating disorders at different stages of life. For example, they may develop anorexia as teenagers but face

Opposite: People can live healthy, happy, active lives in recovery from eating disorders.

bulimia or binge eating when they are older. Some patients prefer to say they are "in recovery" forever, even when they seem cured of their eating disorders. This may help them remember to pay attention to their moods and behaviors to avoid relapsing. Doctors at the state-of-the-art Eating Recovery Center in Denver, Colorado, talk about the "rule of thirds": one-third of patients will get better in one to three years, one-third in four to seven years, and one-third will take longer.

Recovery is hard work. It is difficult even under the best of circumstances—when the person with the disorder is willing to accept help and do the work it takes to get better; when that person has the support of family, friends, and knowledgeable doctors; and when that person can afford the financial and time costs of treatment. Sometimes the layers of treatment that need to happen counteract each other. For example, people with anorexia may have weakened bones. Exercise helps to rebuild bones and improve overall health, but if exercise is going to delay a person putting weight back on, it may not be a good idea to prioritize it. Still, medical experts say that eating disorders do not have to last a lifetime. People can, and do, recover from them.

CHOOSING THE RIGHT TREATMENT

Experts agree: the first step in treating eating disorders is getting the patient to a weight that is normal and healthy for that person. Eating disorders are mental disorders. However, the brain cannot be treated if it is not being fueled with nutrients from food. A patient must be eating properly for their brain to work well enough to respond to therapy.

No matter what other choices a patient makes, treatment will likely begin with a physical exam, a meeting with a mental health professional, and lab tests checking for blood count, electrolytes, organ function, bone density, and heart irregularities. These exams are important because they not only tell doctors where a patient is starting but they also give that patient an idea of where they need to go to be healthy. There are tests that measure how much energy their body uses for everyday functions as well as while being physically active. Knowing this helps doctors set meal plans.

Types of Treatment Locations

There are several different treatment locations. Medical professionals help each patient determine which is best for them in their unique situation. One is not better or worse than another. The right choice is the one that fits the patient's physical and mental health needs.

Patients who are relatively physically and mentally stable may be able to complete treatment through an outpatient center. That means they have individual appointments with doctors and therapists and continue to live at home, not in a hospital or treatment center, and go to school or work.

Partial hospitalization or day treatment is a unique transition service for patients who need more than outpatient treatment but less than full hospitalization. It is also useful for patients leaving treatment—attending a partial hospitalization program can help them transition back to living life full time in the world. Patients spend all day, every day at treatment, returning home only to sleep each night.

Residential and inpatient programs both require the patient to live 24/7 at the treatment facility. The difference between the two is intensity and location. A person who enters residential treatment needs

Dr. Margherita Mascolo is the lead doctor at the ACUTE Center for Eating Disorders, part of Denver Health Medical Center.

constant professional mental health support but is medically stable. Inpatient treatment is more intense, with careful monitoring, and happens at a hospital because the patient is so physically sick that their life may be in jeopardy.

Types of Treatment

Just as a person should choose a treatment facility based on their unique needs, they should choose a type of therapy also based on individual needs. Different therapies work differently for different people. A patient is never alone in this choice—parents and doctors will help. It may be a good idea to first consider evidence-based treatments. These are treatments that have been shown through research to help people with eating disorders specifically.

Cognitive behavioral therapy (CBT) helps a person adjust their beliefs, values, and thoughts so that they no longer see disordered eating as the solution to their problems. That is because, with CBT, the patient comes to understand that their attitudes toward their weight and appearance are distorted and false. There is evidence that CBT is effective for those with bulimia and binge eating disorder.

Cognitive remediation therapy (CRT) is being studied to see how it helps patients with anorexia. CRT breaks down the rigid thinking processes that people with anorexia have. Patients learn to think with open minds about food and their bodies.

There is evidence that dialectical behavior therapy (DBT) is useful in treating binge eating disorder, bulimia, and anorexia. In this therapy, the focus is on developing behaviors to take the place of disordered eating behaviors. These new skills include mindful eating, creating deeper friendships, and learning positive ways to cope with stress.

Interpersonal psychotherapy (IPT) recognizes that bulimia and binge eating disorder occur within a social and interpersonal context, so improving that context will help treat the eating disorders. IPT helps clients improve relationships with friends, family, and teachers.

Psychodynamic psychotherapy asks patients to think about the reasons why they behave the way they do. If they can address these motivations, the habits will change. For people with eating disorders, changing habits around food and eating is one of the ways they can return to a healthy weight.

Family-based treatment (FBT) works for many teens with anorexia and bulimia. It is also called the Maudsley Method or Maudsley Approach. It does not focus on the cause of the eating disorder—anxiety

Families may want to work on treatment together in family therapy.

or depression, for example. Instead, the patient and their family work first on getting the patient's weight back to a healthy number. All family members participate in this treatment. They may even directly feed the patient. Together, they reestablish healthy eating patterns.

There is a genetic component to eating disorders, and family members with disordered eating habits can negatively influence each other. However, families can just as strongly affect patients in a positive direction as well. Cynthia Bulik, a researcher from the University of North Carolina, Chapel Hill, called families the "best allies" in treatment and recovery. Parents, and sometimes even siblings and members of the extended family, must be involved in a patient getting healthy.

Family members help each other be healthy eaters when they approach meals without judgment. Someone is not a "good person" if they eat one thing and a "bad person" if they eat another.

They should highlight the importance of self-esteem over body-esteem. If a parent compliments their teen's appearance, they should also compliment the teen's great joke-telling at dinner the night before or say they are also really impressed by the teen's recent test scores in math. All family members can practice this with each other. It is important not to make fun of each other's looks and also to celebrate other personal qualities. Families love each other for lots of reasons, and showing that love helps prevent eating disorders.

Choosing and Preparing to Meet a Doctor

Therapists, nurses, and doctors are here to help you. You first need to find the right doctor for you. You may want to start by talking with your general practitioner about what you are feeling and your eating habits. Or you may start by finding a mental health therapist. You then need to provide that therapist with detailed information, so they can understand you enough to help you. Ask your parents to help you with this.

Each state arranges its mental health services differently, as does each health insurance company and health insurance plan. One way to find a doctor is to ask your friends if they like theirs. Then talk to your parents to see if your insurance covers those doctors. You can also talk with your general practitioner. Chances are, if they recommend a therapist, that therapist will be nearby and covered by your insurance.

If you cannot find a mental health doctor near you or you cannot get an appointment soon enough, look into online or phone options. Some therapy is available through video chats or phone calls. If your family does not have health insurance, talk with doctors about sliding-scale fees. You can also visit the website for the National Association of Free and Charitable Clinics.

You and your parents may want to interview therapists. It is OK to ask therapists to explain what

Shawn Johnson's Story

Shawn Johnson won Olympic gold in gymnastics when she was sixteen years old and came in second on television's *Dancing with the Stars* when she was twenty. She is both a world-class athlete and a mainstream celebrity. She also is an example of how eating disorders can happen to anyone, even people who do not look like they have one.

Gymnast Shawn Johnson reacted to world-class stress by developing an eating disorder.

As an athlete, Johnson had little body fat, but she "looked bigger" because of her muscles. She felt she was falling short of gymnastic judges' expectations of thinness. At twelve, Johnson was training for the Olympics, and she restricted her calorie intake severely.

After her success at the Olympics, Johnson felt less performance pressure and started eating better. However, when she competed on *Dancing with the Stars*, she became a target for body-shaming on social media. She tried to lose weight fast, this time with diet pills and juice cleanses. That led her to feel sadder, which led to renewed weight-loss attempts, which led to more unhappiness.

Though she never went to a doctor about her eating, Johnson believes she had a disorder and would have performed better in her sport if she had been eating healthier. She finally found help by opening up to her loved ones and working with a nutritionist.

their preferred therapy is, what a typical session is like, and how many patients with eating disorders they help.

Before you go to a pediatrician or therapist about your mental health and eating, think carefully about what you have been experiencing. Try to answer as many of the following questions as you can, because this information will help your doctor help you.

- What do you do that worries you?
- When did this start?
- How often do you engage in behaviors related to your eating disorder?
- How long does each episode last?
- What is going on in your life when the episodes happen?
- How do you feel during and after?
- If you are answering these questions for a first meeting with a therapist, what information from your general practitioner visits can you share?

When you go to meet with a therapist, remember that it is all right if you two are not a good match. You want the best doctor for you, and the doctor wants to be able to help you in the best way possible. Meet with the therapist at least twice. After that, if the appointments do not feel helpful to you, talk with your parents. Tell them what is not working for you and discuss if there are other options you can try.

HELPING LOVED ONES

Mental Health First Aid (mentalhealthfirstaid.org) is like CPR for the brain. Even people with no medical training can learn CPR and then help someone having a heart attack until paramedics arrive. People who learn Mental Health First Aid use a five-step process to help people having a mental health crisis until medical professionals can take over.

This training is not geared toward eating disorders specifically. It does train people to help those experiencing depression, anxiety, and substance use, conditions that people with eating disorders also often have. Mental Health First Aiders learn how to listen without judgment and with compassion, give comfort, provide information about self-help techniques like meditation, and help the person in crisis identify resources that could help them more. Visit the organization's website to learn about training courses.

Teen Health Week is another resource. It offers trustworthy information and programs to help teenagers be proactive in their mental and physical health. The program started in 2016 and is held every spring. Mental health has its own day during the week. Teen Health Week started as an official Pennsylvania statewide health initiative, but now there are events around the country and the globe. You can find out how to get involved by following @teenhealthweek on Twitter and Instagram and going to the website https://collegeofphysicians.org/thw.

MAKE A CRISIS PLAN AND SPEAK UP

A crisis plan will help people with eating disorders stay safe. They can keep a copy with them, and their loved ones can keep copies too. These plans may include information such as this:

- Contact information for therapists and other health-care providers
- Contact information for crisis or helplines
- Contact information for family members or friends who would be helpful in a crisis
- Diagnosis and any medications
- Information about previous mental health crises or emergencies
- History of drug use
- Triggers
- Things that have helped in the past

Medical professionals offer crucial support to those suffering from eating disorders—during a crisis

Resources to Contact for Help

IN AN EMERGENCY

If you or someone you know is in immediate danger, call 911, day or night. Tell the person who answers that there is a psychiatric emergency. Ask for a police officer trained in crisis intervention or trained to help people experiencing a mental health emergency.

DURING A CRISIS

If you or someone you know is not in immediate danger but cannot wait to talk to a trained counselor, contact a 24/7 crisis phone or text helpline. These crisis workers will help you feel safe and help you identify options for further counseling. These discussions are confidential and free.

National Suicide Prevention Lifeline

800-273-TALK (8255)

National Alliance on Mental Illness Crisis Text Line

Text "NAMI" to 741741

FOR GENERAL HELP

If you are not experiencing an emergency or a crisis, but you would like to speak with a trained volunteer about what you are experiencing or ask for referrals to treatment programs, you can contact a helpline. These volunteers are available only certain hours, so pay attention to what time zone they work in.

National Alliance on Mental Illness

800-950-NAMI (6264)

info@nami.org

Monday–Friday 10:00 a.m.–6:00 p.m. Eastern Time Zone

National Association of Anorexia Nervosa and Associated Disorders

650-577-1330

Monday-Friday 9:00 a.m.–5:00 p.m. Central Time Zone

or emergency as well as during ongoing, day-to-day treatment. However, no doctor, therapist, or first responder is perfect. Teens with eating disorders and their parents should listen to medical professionals and also advocate for themselves.

Some professionals still think eating disorders are a choice, so they may not prioritize treating these patients. Some professionals still think teen boys and young men are not at risk for eating disorders. Those patients may go through unnecessary tests or be misdiagnosed. In those cases, teens and parents need to speak up or maybe change doctors.

LOOKING TO THE FUTURE

The future of treatment of eating disorders is exciting. Experts are starting to integrate the cutting-edge brain research they are doing into treatment techniques. For example, it is common to reward a patient who makes progress. However, because it seems that brains vulnerable to eating disorders respond better to consequence than reward, treatment facilities are starting to guide patients that way. If a patient does not eat their meal, they may lose a privilege like being able to wear their favorite outfit, or they may be moved to a stricter ward in the hospital.

Some treatment centers combine this new knowledge with modern technology. Patients at the Eating Recovery Center wear armband sensors that track their calories in and out. If they look at the displays on their biofeedback finger probes, they can see their heart rate and body temperature. Both of these help them see when they are staying on their doctor-prescribed course and when they are veering into dangerous territory. When they listen to their body's distress signs, they can take immediate steps to help themselves.

The center also uses old-fashioned techniques, like flexibility training, to address modern-day research about brains. Doctors working with victims of traumatic brain injury have long used this flexibility training to help their patients. Since we are beginning to understand that the brains of people with eating disorders are hardwired to encourage disordered eating, mental health doctors at ERC have borrowed flexibility training techniques. They ask their patients to do everyday actions in slightly different ways. For example, if they always pick up their phone with their right hand, they should use their left. If they always sit by the window, they should sit by the door. This disrupts habit, which physically changes the brain and interrupts the thoughts that allow for unhealthy eating.

The more we know about eating disorders, the less stigma will surround them because we will not have to rely on misinformation or outdated stereotypes. Families and friends can be more supportive because they will know what kind of help works best. Patients will be able to move on with their lives. The future is bright.

Glossary

amenorrhea Not having a period.

anemia Not having enough red blood cells.

anorexia nervosa A diagnosable condition characterized by eating very little and losing a lot of weight.

binge eating disorder (BED) A diagnosable condition characterized by eating an unusually large amount in a set period of time.

body dysmorphic disorder (BDD) A diagnosable condition characterized by an unhealthy focus on a slight or imagined body "flaw."

bulimia nervosa A diagnosable condition characterized by purging after eating.

cisgender Having a gender identity that matches the sex identified at birth.

Cures Act Formally known as The 21st Century Cures Act; the first US federal law to recognize eating disorders as a mental health issue.

cyberbullying Mean messages toward a person or group of people that are posted online or sent via text message.

***Diagnostic and Statistical Manual of Mental Disorders, Fifth Edition* (DSM-5)** The American Psychiatric Association's reference book that doctors and researchers use to diagnose mental disorders, including eating disorders.

electrolyte imbalance When the body has abnormal amounts of nutrients such as potassium, sodium, and calcium.

fasting Not eating.

interpersonal psychotherapy (IPT) Therapy that links a patient's mood and disturbing life events in order to treat the mood.

muscle dysmorphia A diagnosable condition characterized by an obsession with being muscular.

normative discontent The idea that it is normal for females to feel unhappy about their weight.

orthorexia An obsession with eating healthy foods.

osteopenia Having less bone density than is healthy.

other specified feeding or eating disorders (OSFED) Conditions that have not been officially classified as eating disorders but that cause serious concern, have symptoms similar to classified mental illnesses, and should be treated.

regurgitate After swallowing, to bring food up again into the mouth.

spon con Sponsored content; advertisements.

stressor Something that causes a person stress.

transgender Having a gender identity that does not match the sex identified at birth.

trigger Something that causes an intense, negative emotional response in a person.

Further Information

BOOKS

Barson, K. A. *45 Pounds (More or Less)*. New York: The Penguin Group, 2014.

Brady, Shari. *It's Not What You're Eating, It's What's Eating You: A Teenager's Guide to Preventing Eating Disorders—And Loving Yourself*. New York: Skyhorse Publishing, 2018.

Taylor, Julia V. *The Body Image Workbook for Teens: Activities to Help Girls Develop a Healthy Body Image in an Image-Obsessed World*. Oakland, CA: Instant Help Books, 2014.

WEBSITES

Born This Way Foundation

https://bornthisway.foundation

Founded by Lady Gaga and her mother, Cynthia Germanotta, the Born This Way Foundation offers resources and research related to the wellness of young people and helps them act in positive ways.

Project HEAL

https://www.theprojectheal.org

Started by two fifteen-year-olds in 2008, this advocacy group for people with eating disorders offers lots of volunteer, intern, and mentor opportunities.

VIDEOS

Inside the Eating Disordered Mind

https://www.youtube.com/watch?time_continue=352&v=DJo4OWtpcYU

In this video from the National Eating Disorders Association, several young people talk about their experiences with eating disorders and how they look ahead to the future.

Teen Eating Disorders and Residential Treatment—Her Story

https://www.youtube.com/watch?v=S6V3keFXbFY&feature=youtu.be

A teen talks about how her eating disorder affected her life and what treatment and recovery was like.

Bibliography

Center for Discovery. "Eating Disorder Statistics." Accessed on November 15, 2018. http://www.centerfordiscoveryportland.com/eating-disorder-research/eating-disorder-statistics.

Cowden, Susan. "Media Influence on Eating." Verywell Mind, February 8, 2018. https://www.verywellmind.com/media-influence-on-disordered-eating-1138266.

Dotinga, Randy. "Many Women with Eating Disorders Do Recover, Study Finds." *Chicago Tribune*, January 24, 2017. https://www.chicagotribune.com/lifestyles/health/ct-many-with-eating-disorders-get-better-health-0125-20170124-story.html.

Goldberg, Haley. "Congress Just Passed the First Eating Disorder Legislation." *Self*, December 9, 2016. https://www.self.com/story/congress-just-passed-the-first-ever-eating-disorder-legislation.

Harris, Kristin. "PLL Star Troian Bellisario Gets Super-Personal in Our Exclusive Interview!" *Seventeen*, January 6, 2014. https://www.seventeen.com/celebrity/movies-tv/g701/troian-bellisario-quotes/#slide-1.

Moura, Sophie. "Starvation Nation: Inside a Groundbreaking Eating Disorder Facility." *Marie Claire*, June 20, 2011. https://www.marieclaire.com/health-fitness/news/a6229/eating-disorder-facility.

National Alliance on Mental Illness. "Eating Disorders." Accessed on November 15, 2018. https://www.nami.org/Learn-More/Mental-Health-Conditions/Eating-Disorders.

National Eating Disorders Association. "Eating Disorder Myths." Accessed on November 15, 2018. https://www.nationaleatingdisorders.org/toolkit/parent-toolkit/eating-disorder-myths.

National Institute of Mental Health. "Eating Disorders." Accessed on November 15, 2018. https://www.nimh.nih.gov/health/topics/eating-disorders/index.shtml.

O'Toole, Julie. "Anorexia Nervosa Case Report, Circa 1684." Kartini Clinic, December 23, 2011. https://www.kartiniclinic.com/blog/post/anorexia-nervosa-case-report-circa-1684.

Shaw, Gina. "Anorexia: The Body Neglected." WebMD. Last updated October 2018. https://www.webmd.com/mental-health/eating-disorders/anorexia-nervosa/features/anorexia-body-neglected.

Index

Page numbers in **boldface** refer to images.

About the Author

Kristin Thiel is a writer from Portland, Oregon. She has written numerous books on topics ranging from science and technology, to biographies, to history and current affairs. Thiel is the author of *Helping Yourself, Helping Others: Dealing with Teen Pregnancy*.